WRESTLING
with
RHYME

The Hulkster

WRESTLING

with

RHYME

By

LANNY POFFO

LEILO

Designed and produced
by Frank DeMaio

"LEAPING LANNY": WRESTLING WITH RHYME

PRINTING HISTORY
Leilo Publications edition published 1988

Illustrations by Lynne Gutshall.

For information address: Leilo Publications, 13300 Indian Rocks Road #2103, Largo, FL 34644

ISBN: 0-9619169-0-7

Library of Congress #87-51044

PRINTED IN THE UNITED STATES OF AMERICA

10 9 8 7 6 5 4 3 2 1

DEDICATION

TO PAT

They said she had six months to live
But she was in the hands of God
Not just the lab report of some physician
Now many years have come and gone
And I just saw her yesterday
She told me her disease was in remission

My fifth grade teacher means so much
To me and several hundred more
Who witnessed her courageous walk of faith
When God created each of us
The seventh day he rested
Just to come back even stronger on the
  eighth

She's been teaching by example
At Pierce Downer School and Puffer
And many lives have changed because of
  that
I knew her as Miss Rufenacht
But she is Mrs. Mochel now
So I'll just dedicate my book "To Pat"

CONTENTS

Introduction 9

Part One: In the Ring

Chapter 1: Personal Wrestling Collection 19

Chapter 2: Wrestling Stars 29

Chapter 3: WrestleMania Collection 87

Chapter 4: Wrestling Announcers 97

Chapter 5: Wrestling Arenas 107

Part Two: Out of the Ring

Chapter 1: Charities 115

Chapter 2: Children's Hospitals 121

Chapter 3: Silly Stuff 127

Chapter 4: Serious Stuff 137

Chapter 5: My Private Collection 159

INTRODUCTION

DIVERSITY

A book of wrestling poetry
So fans of every age
Can get to know their favorite stars
But *not* on every page

My diversity of topics
You may find to be absurd
But you'll find *something* that you like
Of this I give my word

AN APOLOGY TO ROBERT PENN WARREN

For 80 million wrestling fans
I am the "Poet Laureate"
And for that title I apologize
For Robert Warren is the man
Who represents the USA
And I am quite embarrassed by the lies

But if my verses make you smile
Or make you feel a certain feeling
Just enough to make you think again
Then I'm a very happy man
No matter what the critics say
For I am just as proud as Robert's pen

WRESTLING *with* RHYME

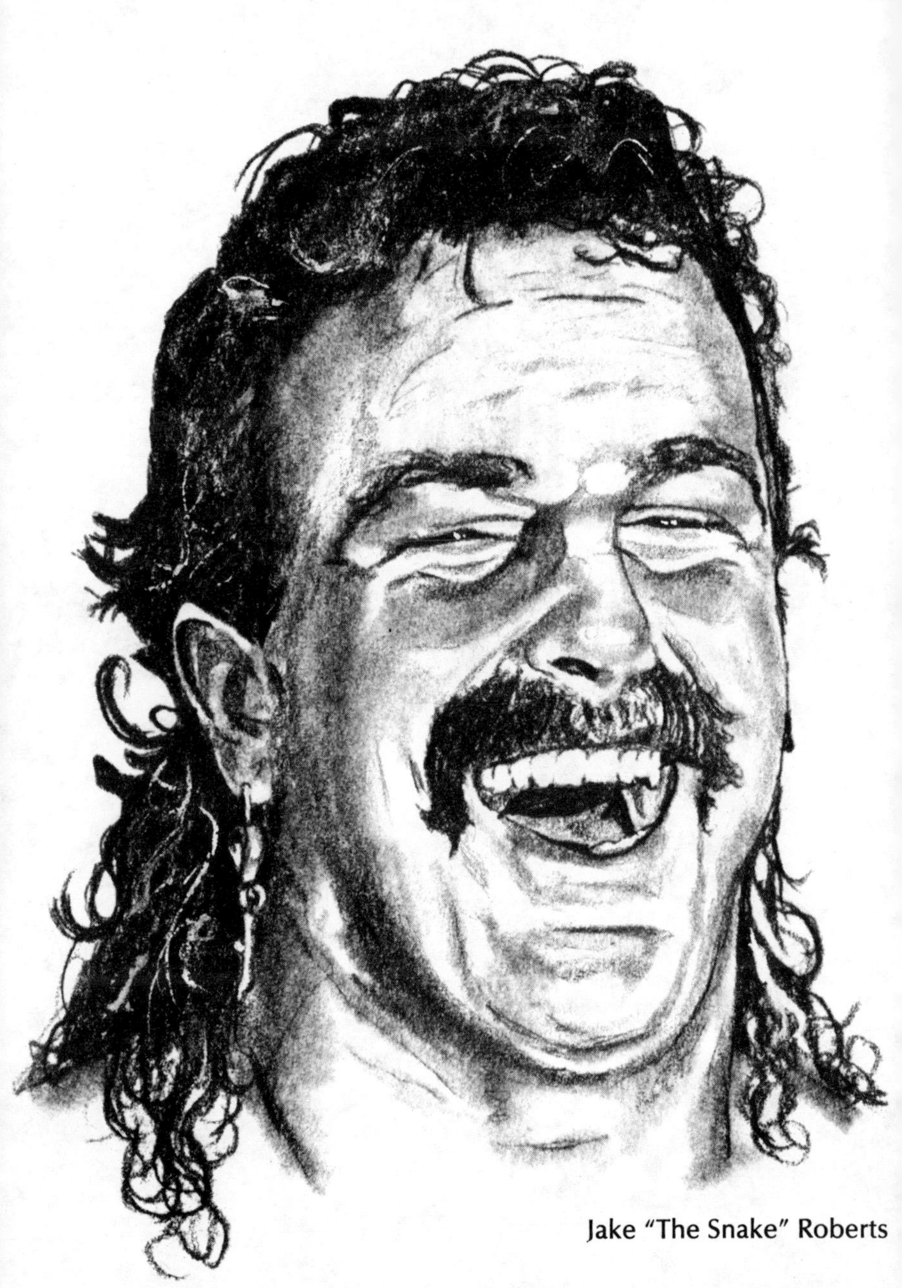

Jake "The Snake" Roberts

PART ONE

IN THE RING

Randy "Macho Man" Savage

CHAPTER 1

PERSONAL WRESTLING COLLECTION

BEFORE THE BELL

Before this wrestling match begins
I have some words to say
To fans from every nation
And throughout the USA

It wasn't very long ago
I had a ringside seat
My father was a champion
Who seldom knew defeat

I'd pray each night to God above
If I could pay my dues
That I could be a wrestler too
And fill my father's shoes

World Wrestling Federation
The answer to my prayer
My father's watching every move
My opponent best beware

FAITH

Some say the pen can beat the sword
While others disagree
To hedge my bets I carry both
As you can plainly see

It's *faith* that moves that mountain
Much more than strength or speed
The greatest tree in the forest
Was once a tiny seed

World Wrestling Federation
Three words that mean a lot
And if my best is good enough
I'll give it all I've got

CHIVALRY LIVES

Look back through the annals of history
And the Wrestling Hall of Fame
Men from all nations with courage to spare
Who struggled to carve out a name

Now compare these high standards of valor
To those chivalrous Knights of yore
With bravery as staunch as their armor
Their glory both legend and lore

My medieval connection with wrestling
Relives that magnificent past
Though mindless skeptics may snicker and scoff
The winner is he who laughs last

TNT

Alive with the love of wrestling
I appear on TNT
Between Vince, and "Awful Alfred"
The hottest show on TV

I'm not your average wrestler
But, I wouldn't want to be
I never scream, or kiss my arms
I'm happy, just being me

I call myself "Leaping Lanny"
I validate what I say
To every single wrestling fan
Who's watching "USA"

Yes, I believe in miracles
As God has blessed this great land
I believe the referee
Will soon be raising my hand!

CULTURE SHOCK

The World Wrestling Federation
Has caused a culture shock
In every phase of our society
From classical to rock

In triumphant jubilation
Every social class is one
With a single common interest
Just to have a little fun

I've seen the rapture in the eyes
Of fans from every nation
You made us what we are today
World Wrestling Federation

AUTOGRAPH

When I was just a little "Leap"
I'd try to get an autograph
Of all the greatest wrestlers of the time
Well, some of them weren't all that bad
But some were too important
And I knew right then and there, that was a crime

Fame is just a fleeting thing
And if you let it swell your head
Life has a way to take you down a notch
So many times I've seen a bum
Who used to live in glory
It's been that way since Hackenschmidt lost to
  Gotch*

It really doesn't take much time
To sign a piece of paper
And time is never wasted on a youth
We're equal in the eyes of God
In spite of our publicity
(I'll bet He's not impressed, to tell the truth)

*First recognized World Heavyweight Wrestling match

NICE GUYS

If you think nice guys finish last
You're making a mistake
The biggest winners are the ones
Who give more than they take

Hulk Hogan takes his vitamins
Works out and says his prayers
And does a lot of special things
To please the man upstairs

You still think nice guys finish last?
You'd better just think twice
It's nice to be important
But more important to be nice

I have had some disappointments
That I like to call injustice
But they cannot take the smile from my face
For I have never lost a match
In 15 years of wrestling
Because I prefer to call it "second place"

Anything that doesn't kill me
Serves to make me strong as steel
(Which, as everybody knows, is forged in flame)
Andrew Carnegie could tell you
But since he is not around
He has left this world with more than when he came

For God has answered all my prayers
In ways, although mysterious,
Has left me with a lofty sense of worth
I can feel His love around me
Even though I'm just a drop
In the ocean, on this tiny planet Earth

CHAPTER 2

WRESTLING STARS

KOKO B. WARE

There's a new kid in town name of Koko B. Ware
And that name ought to put you in line
You may think that his dancing is just for the birds
But his wrestling is sweeter than wine

Those incredible legs take him high off the ground
'Til he's hang gliding up in the air
When he kicks you so hard that your toes curl up
You have learned why they call him B. Ware

The Hulkste

HULKAMANIA

When the Hulkster hits the ring
That's when it hits the fan
A nuclear explosion
From a modern Superman

There never is an empty seat
They line up in the rain
Not even Halley's Comet
Could make the fans refrain

In the magic of the moment
When the action gets intense
Kids from 6 to 86
Are raptured with suspense

There has never been a hero
Of such magnitude before
He's been the champ for three years now
And here's to many more!

Bruno Sammartino

THE LIVING LEGEND

Once upon a Wrestling ring
But not so long ago
Mr. Bruno Sammartino
Was the only name to know

He stood up to Buddy Rogers
And the "nature boy" went down
Less than 60 seconds later
Sammartino wore the crown

He's the real "Italian Stallion"
That's a fact you can't ignore
His career had more success
Than Rocky I, II, III and IV

The Living Legend lives again
For every single fan
He's on the microphone each week
Right next to Vince McMahon

MOOLAH!

Since we're on the subject of legends
Who are still alive and well
I could fill another book or two
'bout a poor little southern belle

Her first job was a cotton field
In the Carolina sun
She picked a hundred pounds each day
And she thought of it as fun

She was just a little girl of nine
But she was nobody's fool
She was cashing in at a penny a pound
And working her way through school

The Fabulous Moolah has paid her dues
On the road to fame and glory
She's a real American Classic
Horatio Alger story

DAVID'S DILEMMA

The name of Sammartino
  really packs a lot of weight
For Bruno of the good ol' days
  and David as of late

Nostalgic happy memories
  of once upon a time
For several million Bruno fans
  the past is so sublime

For Bruno Sammartino
  was a hero to us all
When I grew up I had his picture
  hanging on my wall

Imagine all those people
  watching David's every move
The son of Sammartino
  has an awful lot to prove

I've seen David flatten his opponent
  quick as 1, 2, 3
But they still say Bruno's greater
  than his son will ever be

The shadow David wrestles in
  is on his back like glue
To fill his father's shoes
  would be impossible to do

The Sammartino legacy
  is very hard to take
But David tries the best he can
  so give the kid a break

THE JUNKYARD DOG

Ladies and gentlemen, boys and girls
I hope I don't offend you
But thinkin' about that Junk Yard Dog
Puts soul food on the menu!

Who dat walkin' down the aisle
And flash dat million dollar smile
His eyes aglow with love and lust
And another one bites the dust

The Junk Yard Dog is so much fun
And some folks say he's #1
He's big and black and bad and bold
With nerves of steel and heart of gold

He's from the hungry side of town
But no one dares to put him down
He's generating so much soul
The wrestling fans just lose control

But even though he does his thing
He's still all business in the ring
The Junk Yard Dog is very smart
Look what he's done to Jimmy Hart

He took that branding iron away
And messed up Jimmy's little "A"
So Grab Them Cakes and come and see
The one and only "JYD"

BILLY JACK'S BEST HOLD

Billy Jack's from Oregon
Where rain and sun make trees
That's why he proudly wears the green and gold
Well, that explains the color scheme
But what's behind his piercing eyes
Is stronger than his favorite wrestling hold

His father is his biggest fan
He's blind and needs a lot of rest
But wrestling's on his television dial
When Billy Jack's victorious
Just close your eyes and concentrate
And you can almost feel his father smile

George "The Animal" Steel
and Dr. Ruth

GEORGE STEELE

Whose appetite for turnbuckles
  is making all that mess
The man who has to sweep the ring
  will give you just one guess

They call George Steele the "Animal"
  but take a closer look
The cover doesn't indicate
  the beauty in this book

His passion for Elizabeth's
  in vain to say the least
But the beauty has compassion
  for this broken-hearted beast

The reaction of the "Macho Man"
  has really been uncouth
We need Joyce Brothers and Dear Abby,
  and maybe Dr. Ruth!

SANTANA'S REVENGE

I would like to tell the story
of a dedicated man
Who overcame an injury,
delighting every fan
His name is Tito Santana,
from ol' Mexico to you
He planned to win his title back
though some said he was through

A wrestler's knees are critical
the doctors know that well
When they performed the surgery
no one would dare foretell
That he could rehabilitate
and train through constant pain
When he challenged Greg the Hammer
many thought he was insane

One magic night in Baltimore
they called his chances bad
But learned what Tito's people call
¡Un momento de verdad!
The moment of truth was destiny
victorious in the end
And I am very proud to say
Santana is my friend

SUPERSTAR BILLY GRAHAM

No mercy in the desert
In the Arizona sun
You either move, adapt, or burn away
But look at Billy Graham
His eyes are scorched with fire
And the ravages of every single ray

His muscles, how they smolder
And when he turns on the heat
He just leaves the other wrestlers in the cold
And I respect the "Superstar"
Because he's so authentic
In a world where all that glitters is not gold

KEN PATERA

We know Ken Patera got in trouble in Wisconsin
And we know why he had to go to jail
But now he's free and seems to have a different attitude
And Bobby Heenan's looking rather pale
This great Olympic Champion has payback on his mind
And Bobby Heenan's smile has turned to fear
Ken Patera shocked the Wrestling World with this announcement
That "Weasel Hunting" season now is here

BRUTUS THE BARBER

Just look at "Luscious Johnny V"
You know why he's a flop?
His "Dream Team" has to pay their dues
At "Beefcake's Barber Shop"

Brutus "The Barber" Beefcake

Hillbilly Jim

HILLBILLY JIM

From the foothills of Kentucky
pioneered by Daniel Boone
Comes a rompin' stompin' hero
hotter than the month of June

He was discovered by Hulk Hogan
just a diamond in the rough
Hillbilly Jim is not a quitter
when the rasslin' gets too tough

But from the streets of San Francisco
comes a man who don't seem right
and they call him Brutus Beefcake
but you ought to see him fight

Johnny Valiant made the challenge
putting both men on the limb
One night in San Diego
saw the end of Hillbilly Jim

Pro Wrestling is a battlefield
and danger signs our checks
For what they've done to big Jim's leg
I hope he breaks their necks

Father Time's the greatest healer
Jim will take some if he's smart
Just remember what was damaged
was his leg and not his heart

When the Hulkster takes his vitamins
works out and says his prayers
You can bet Big Jim gets mentioned
to the big man way upstairs

IVAN PUTSKI

When Ivan Putski hits the ring
The fans get quite a thrill
He cuts opponents down to size
Then goes in for the kill

With a maximum of muscle
And not a trace of fat
Just like the map in bold relief
He shows you where it's at

To be chosen as his partner
Has been my finest hour
It's not another Polish joke
I'm talking "Polish Power!"

LADY WRESTLING

When "Sensational Sherry" wrestled Velvet
McIntyre
Lady Wrestling had been raised to lofty heights
Chauvinistic pigs, and men of similar description
Were converted to the cause of equal rights

Looking and behaving with a dignified appeal
Metamorphosis occurred right at the bell
Outside the ring these ladies were polite and shy
and so demure
But in the ring, they really fought like hell!

To judge the universal by particular example
Is the basis of all racist/sexist views
You male ego maniacs should step into the ring
And just *try* to fill these ladies' wrestling shoes

CORPORAL KIRSCHNER

When you tell Corporal Kirschner
He can take a flying leap
You'd better wipe the smile off your face
He's always jumping out of planes
For good ol' Uncle Sam
And marching up and down his Army base

He has hit the dusty trail
And he's been to hell and back
He's as bad as bad can be right to the bone
He's a real wrestling "Rambo"
So get ready for a fight
Or get out of Corporal Kirschner's combat zone

JIMMY HART

There's a wimpy little manager
with megaphone in hand
Telling lies with great authority
at speed to beat the band
From his television interviews
he thinks he's pretty smart
His big mouth is from the south
and he is known as Jimmy Hart

He laughs at such high frequencies
that dogs for miles away
Would sooner be attending a big
fireworks display
From the laces of his gym shoes
to his pointy little nose
I'm looking for the day when he
starts reaping what he sows

He's a hyperactive manager
who likes to shuck and jive
And he sounds just like an
album being played at 45
The Junkyard Dog exposing Jimmy's
panties on TV
Was the most deserving branding
ever seen on NBC

The manager of the year award
was confidence destroying
It's a shame they didn't have a
prize for this year's most annoying
You will not find Jimmy Hart
wherever peace of mind survives
He's the scratching fingernails on
the blackboard of our lives

THE HART COLLECTION

I

When I face the Hart Foundation
I always grab the mike
And call these three palookas
All the names that people like

Well, tonight's a different story
Jimmy Hart is such a mess
With lipstick on his collar
And Adonis on his breath

II

When Jim "the Anvil" Neidhart
Teams with Bret "The Hitman" Hart
Together they're as strong as bulls
But only half as smart

III

The Jimmy Hart Foundation
Has an awful lot to prove
The Hitman and the Anvil
Have a plan

They watch the British Bulldogs
And they chart their every move
To take away their titles
If they can

Their muscles are intimidating
From the very start
Determination courses
Through their veins

They dream of being champions
And have a lot of heart
But the three of them together
Have no brains

SLICK

Classie Freddie Blassie took a big load off his mind
With Hercules and Volkoff and the Sheik
But Slick has all the qualities that Freddy's looking
  for
He has a pencil neck and he's a geek

Randy "Macho Man" Savag
and Elizabeth

MACHO MAN'S MANAGER

The number one free agent in the wrestling world today
Has every single manager in total disarray

With Heenan, Fuji, Jimmy Hart and Freddie Blassie too
Even Skaaland and Albano are deciding what to do

But Randy Savage is the man who must decide alone
To get some rest, the Macho Man must disconnect his phone

With eyes inflamed by who knows what he grabs the mike to say
I've come to my decision clear the aisle and stay away

And now the door is open and we break our necks to see
Elizabeth walk from the door to wrestling history

Her face is like a movie star's her figure's nothing less
And Adonis drips with jealousy at every pretty dress

She brings charisma to the ring and keeps his ego fed
And validates his prophecy that Hulkamania's dead!

MR. WONDERFUL

I just saw Mr. Wonderful
And he is looking great
He's handsome, tan and muscular
But still can't get a date

With Bobby Heenan at his side
He really thinks he's hot
But getting past the Hulkster
Takes a lot more than he's got!

Paul "Mr. Wonderful" Orndorff

JAKE THE SNAKE

Since Jake the Snake came on the scene
With "Damien" his little friend
The terror of his D.D.T.
Too horrible to comprehend

His laughing eyes are hideous
As he assaults his helpless foe
If evil is his destiny
He's gone as far as he can go

When he uncoils his giant snake
It's worse than any words can tell
More vile than the putrid slime
That decorates the gates of hell

We turn to Ricky Steamboat
For if this man has what it takes
Perhaps the Dragon will return
To rid the wrestling world of snakes

Jake "The Snake" Roberts

LOUSY REVIEWS

When a wrestler's name becomes a household
word through his endeavors
Hollywood producers beat a pathway to his door
Using Captain Lou Albano and the Hulkster as
examples
Fuji and Muraco figured they could handle more

Muraco felt with his good looks he didn't need an
agent
Hollywood's heroic hunks just wouldn't stand a
chance
When they zoomed the camera in he figured that
was all he needed
To fibulate the audience's senses with romance

The best laid plans of mice and men will sometimes
go awry
And there's no fast and easy way to make a million
bucks
If Fuji and Muraco want to make it in this world
They had better stick to wrestling 'cause their acting
really sucks

HERCULES HERNANDEZ

Hercules Hernandez is a mountain of a man
His body is impervious to pain
But all his big decisions he is leaving up to Heenan
That indicates he doesn't have a brain!

So now you doubt my sanity for facing such a man
I realize that he is awfully big
But I came here to fight the odds and score a victory
That ought to make Ventura flip his wig!

KAMALA

It's the Main Event on NBC
The Wrestling World is watching
As Kamala bellies forth upon the scene

But if I emerge victorious
I could be next month's centerfold
In National Geographic Magazine!

Kamala

RAVISHING RICK RUDE

Rick Rude is really ravishing
A picture of perfection
And I'm sure the ladies think he's got it all
Well, I hate to blur the image
But his only love affair
Is with that mirror mirror on the wall

THE KING

He's the self-proclaimed "King of Wrestling"
It's "Handsome" Harley Race
The pages of his great career
Are written on his face

He moves just like a thoroughbred
But *agonizingly* slow
And every devastating move
Destroys his hapless foe

But it takes more than crowns and robes
To fool a wrestling fan
Until this "king" proves otherwise
Hulk Hogan's still the man!

HE'S NO ELVIS

Every single vote is in
And Honky Tonk is out
And Jimmy Hart is smiling with elation
He wants to be like Elvis
But Elvis lives forever
And Honky Tonk's a sorry imitation

BRITISH BULLDOGS

As Winston Churchill said it
still remembered through the years
The only thing I offer you
is blood and sweat and tears

And this spirit that beat Hitler
is it still alive today?
Just watch those "British Bulldogs"
wrestling in the USA

"Davey Boy" and "Dynamite":
now there's a winning hand
They double up and conquer
every tag team in the land

Their heads are on their shoulders
'cause they haven't any necks
Their muscles wear like armor
they don't even have to flex

But when the bell has sounded
just watch those Bulldogs go
The muscles they've been flashin'
well they aren't just for show

They're England's gift to Wrestling
and the fans just dig it all
The way they did for Ringo
and George and John and Paul!

KILLER BEES

I've heard about the Killer B's
But I did not believe
Until I saw Brunzell and Blair
And what was up their sleeve

They have a sense of humor
And they wear it in the ring
Be careful not to laugh too hard
They have a deadly sting

Because both boys begin B.B.
(Brunzell, B. Brian Blair)
Ballistically, behavior's bold
Big bullies best beware

DREAM TEAM

Luscious Johnny Valiant talks on
both sides of his face
The way they stole the title
belts was really a disgrace

Now Brutus Beefcake teamed with
Greg "The Hammer" Valentine
Cavort around as champions
while others wait in line

They've been wrestling under
pressure since becoming #1
They've only lost their cool when
Beefcake's stockings had a run

By his own cigar will Lucious Johnny
someday be impaled
While Beefcake gets devoured
and the Hammer's getting nailed

Then some other team will get
to wear the belts around their waist
I just hope that their successors
will exhibit better taste

THE ROUGEAU BROTHERS

The Rougeau family from Montreal
Have been making headlines for many years
Their name has been a symbol of respect
And now it's Raymond and his brother Jacques
Who are keeping family tradition
They give the fans much more than they expect

They have a certain *je ne sais quoi*
And much more than their share of *savoir faire*
To make the pretty young girls say *Ooh-la-la*
What's the question the ladies ask the most
Of the Rougeau brothers, *s'il vous plait*
Voulez-vous coucher avec moi ce soir

THE ISLANDERS

Bobby Heenan and his Islanders are one terrific team
And they're aiming for the top, as you can tell

But just a warning to the Weasel, "You had better watch your step,
And the *Strike Force* of Santana and Martel"

BOBBY HEENAN

Here's my opinion of Bobby the Brain
A title that no one disputes
Though some may call him eccentric or vain
His blond hair not quite like it's roots

But he's never been stuck for an answer
He has held Mean Gene to a draw
His big mouth has the skill of a dancer
Which at times leaves Lord Alfred in awe

He just hates when the fans call him "Weasel"
Now *that* doesn't make *any* sense
Poor little weasels all over the world
Are the ones that *should* take offense

Bobby "The Brain" Heenan

JESSE'S MOVIE

"The Superstars of Wrestling" is a Nielsen delight
And the ratings just get bigger every show
While Vince and Bruno try to give the fans a little
class
Jesse tries to make it "Larry, Curly, Moe!"

I saw him in the "Predator" with Arnold
Schwarzenegger
Jesse's presence made the movie really great
I hope this movie wins him an Academy Award
He's the man the wrestling fans just love to hate!

VOLKOFF AND SHEIK

If Volkoff comes from Russia, and the Sheik comes
from Iran
I have a question on the minds of every single fan

Every time your mouth is open you must put our
country down
If you hate us all so much than tell us why you're
still around

There are many boats and planes that leave our
country every day
And I'd gladly buy two tickets (just as long as they're
one-way)

'cause a lot of people fought and died to make this
country free
And we're sick of seeing both your ugly faces on TV

But I know the real reason you won't leave the USA
Once you've had a taste of freedom, it's so hard to
go away

So with Freddie Blassie at your side, just step into
the ring
And salute your native homelands, as the Russian
starts to sing

And when the bell has sounded and the match is
under way
Some "American inferior" might kick your big red
"A"

"OUTLAW" RON BASS

You see that rugged cowboy with the handlebar mustache?
He's got a couple pounds on me, but I've got more *panache*

That bull whip that he carries leaves a mighty nasty cut
I'd like to take "ol' Betsy" right across his you know what!

TED DIBIASE

Mr. DiBiase has the world at his feet
And if the price is right he'll never fail
Destroying human dignity is how he gets his kicks
But there are still some things in life that aren't for sale

Easy money comes and goes, but there's no satisfaction
Like the feeling of an honest day of work
Lead us not into temptation, but deliver us from evil
Don't you listen to that million dollar jerk

THE STEAMBOAT-MURACO FEUD

The wrestling fans have seen a lot of action through the years
The fans have special memories of happiness and tears

But Fuji and Muraco gave us something to forget
Atrocities that Ricky Steamboat might make them regret

They tied a belt around his throat and almost broke his neck
Then laughed and told the story of how Steamboat hit the deck

The prince of darkness better sleep with only one eye shut
Or else the dragon will return to show them what is what

Then Fuji will not have a place to wear that stupid hat
Magnificent Muraco shall be called much less than that

And several million wrestling fans will stand up on their feet
In praise of Ricky Steamboat whose revenge will be complete

THE FEDERETTES

The Federettes do more than take the jackets from the ring
They create a stunning contrast for the eyes
Their classy brand of pulchritude is getting rave reviews
Three more reasons why the Nielsen Ratings rise

Suzette, Lynette, and Gianette are always on their toes
Because ringside's not the safest place to be
But the Federettes are great at looking pretty under pressure
And they've earned their place in Wrestling History!

RITA MARIE

She's fulfilling the dreams of her brother
Say hello to Rita Marie
Now she's wearing the pants in the wrestling ring
As the first lady referee

But the wrestlers aren't Gloria Steinems
So contempt is thrown right in her face
Like the first black man in the Major Leagues
Who was made to feel out of place

But performance wins out over prejudice
For Jack Tunney and Vince McMahon
When Rita assumes her authority
She's no different than any man

Nobody said "nigger" in Brooklyn
When Robinson beat out the Yanks
The only name they could call him was "sir"
And all they could give him was thanks

Rita's brother has gone to his maker
Jackie Robinson's up there too
On behalf of the people who battle the odds
Rita, we're counting on you

IN PRAISE OF SAM MUCHNICK

Wrestling promoters, more often than not
Retire without any friends
But St. Louis still honors Sam Muchnik
And *nobody* condescends

For all of the years he has given his best
Promoting the "Chase" and the "Kiel"
We pay back Sam Muchnick with love and respect
And that's the way *all* of us feel

PAUL BOESCH

In the tradition of wrestling excellence
That Houston has grown to expect
Paul Boesch is the paragon entrepreneur
That has given us cause to reflect

A soldier, a lifeguard, a wrestler, and more
An announcer, promoter, and ref
Mr. Boesch is the pride of the Lone Star State
And the WWF

WEDDING INVITATION

You're invited to a wedding
From the Meadowlands to you
Uncle Elmer and Joyce Stasko
Have come to say "I do"

Soon the ring will be an altar
And I hope we don't offend
Because God's love is everywhere
And Elmer is my friend

UNCLE ELMER'S WEDDING

On this auspicious occasion
A loving commitment for life
Joyce Stasko and Uncle Elmer
Are united as man and wife

Unselfishly they share their love
With every single wrestling fan
Who supported Uncle Elmer
A wonderful, big hearted man

And we thank them for this moment
So the multitudes may see
The joy of the Holy Spirit
Through the family of NBC

Eros, Philos, Agope
A life of love and wonder
For what God hath joined together
Let no man put asunder

RICK MCGRAW

The death of Rick McGraw
has left the Wrestling world in shock
His life has passed as quickly
as the seconds of a clock

He brightened up a locker room
just walking through the door
I'm sad to say that Rick McGraw
won't do that anymore

Like some ironic tragedy
that no one could foresee
In the spring his wife will have the baby
Rick will never see

We come in this world with nothing
and we leave the way we came
Ashes to ashes and dust to dust
and hallowed be Thy name

His sudden passing is a cross
that all his friends must bear
To those of us who loved this man
the sorrow we must share

I'll remember him quite simply
as a good and decent man
His presence will be dearly missed
by family, friend and fan

The Hulkster
and Randy "Macho Man" Savage

THE HANDSHAKE HEARD 'ROUND THE WORLD

It was the Main Event on NBC from Hershey
Pennsylvania
Where the World watched the birth of "Macho-
Hulkamania"

When lovely Miss Elizabeth was driven to the
wrestling mat
And Honky Tonk took his guitar and used it as a
baseball bat

The circumstances leading to the merging of these
mega powers
Made for such anxiety that all the moments seemed
like hours

But the Macho-Hulkster handshake got a
thunderous ovation
For in it held the future of the World Wrestling
Federation!

CHAPTER 3

WRESTLEMANIA COLLECTION

Jake "The Snake" Robert

PIPER'S LAST HURRAH!

Jimmy Hart and Adrian are planning a surprise
With a pair of scissors and a sleeper hold
If Piper leaves for Hollywood with no hair on his head
They figure his career is going to fold

They have conjured up a scheme to spoil his last hurrah!
And make it hard to find an acting job
I sure hope their plans are thwarted March the 29th
Because Adonis is a fat disgusting slob!

DANNY DAVIS

Danny Davis you're the reason that the Bulldogs
lost their belts
You'll never referee again, you mangy mutt
But we'll all be there in Pontiac on March the 29th
To see you get the stripes knocked off your butt

ANDRE THE GIANT

In this world of wrestling giants
One man puts them all to shame
And he's every bit as rugged
As the Alps from where he came

The French-born Andre Rousimoff 's
No stranger to our shore
But we call him Andre the Giant
'Cause he's every inch and more

And millions stand in line to see
God's mightiest creation
Who's been called the greatest athlete
Of any generation

But he's never had a title shot
And we know very well
Hulk Hogan has a broken heart
And Andre's mad as hell

What will be the Hulk's reply
We'll have to wait and see
'til then we're counting down the days
'til WrestleMania III

WRESTLEMANIA II

It's the hallmark of sports entertainment
And the great American dream come true
The World Wrestling Federation
Is presenting WrestleMania II

King Kong Bundy's alone with Hulk Hogan
The moment of truth when the cage door is shut
And the Hulkster's only chance for revenge
Will be kicking the world's most incredible butt

It's boxing with Piper and Mr. T
And it would be an embarrassing mess
Should Rowdy Roddy get knocked off his feet
Millions of people will look up his dress

It's the football and wrestling connection
A battle royal out of the ordinary
The line of scrimmage is now in the ring
And so is Refrigerator Perry

Los Angeles, New York, and Chicago
Three cities play host to a nation
Life doesn't get any better than this
It's the World Wrestling Federation

AT WRESTLEMANIA II

At the beautiful Rosemont Horizon
The World Wrestling Federation
Is presenting WrestleMania II's
International Celebration

With respect for New York and Los Angeles
Our windy city is on a roll
'cause we haven't put out the Chicago fire
Since the Bears won the Super Bowl

The Hulkster
and Andre the Gian

WRESTLEMANIA III

The Silverdome in Pontiac, on March the 29th
A real World Wrestling celebration
When Andre and the Hulk collide you'll need a Richter Scale
To measure the enormous devastation

The Giant's never been defeated in his great career
And his reputation's far beyond reproach
The fans think Bobby Heenan's just a sneaky little weasel
But to me, he's just another common roach!

The Hulkster's never run away from anyone before
March 29th will be his toughest test
The largest crowd in history will witness every move
It's the battle of the biggest and the best!

Hello world, and welcome to the famous
Silverdome
It's a record crowd, both live, and on TV

We're all a part of history on Sunday afternoon
Because we're all a part of WrestleMania III

CHAPTER 4

WRESTLING ANNOUNCERS

"MEAN GENE" OKERLUND

It's Mr. "Mean Gene" Okerlund
The master of the microphone
The man whose voice has launched a million fans
With pear-shaped tones and resonance
And lightning quick rebuttals
He can hold the wrestling world in his hands

Although he uses fancy words
With "William Buckley" tendencies
He's always good for some atrocious pun
The next time he expostulates
Just get your dictionary
And proceed to have a plethora of fun

Jesse "The Body" Ventura

JESSE'S BODY SHOP

I'm this week's guest on "Body Shop"
Although I don't know why
All Jesse does is flex his arms
A weekly lullaby

But muscle is his calling card
He's every inch a man
He served us well in Viet Nam
While many others ran

So let him flash his pythons
And wear that feathered thing
The only time I'll put him down
Is when we're in the ring

MONSOON AND VENTURA

Jesse "the Body" Ventura and his partner "Gorilla Monsoon"
Have about as much in common as December has with June
And the World Wrestling Federation has them on the air
And television's never seen a more unlikely pair

You will never see the "Body" with the same sunglasses twice
His priority of fashion's to be sure his arms look nice
While Monsoon looks more traditional in formal evening wear
He displays an insight of the ring that's quite beyond compare

Jesse plays the devil's advocate in trashy flashy threads
While Monsoon's vocabulary's over everybody's heads
The intellectual Gorilla doesn't have to feel alone
'cause Jesse has a quite perverted genius of his own

Their philosophies on Wrestling wars are really poles apart
They're in eternal disagreement when they're speaking from the heart
Like when Madison and Felix Unger tried to share a room
This "odd couple" of the microphone makes Nielsen ratings ZOOM!

MONSOON AND HEENAN

Gorilla Monsoon has been sharing the mike
With the infamous "Bobby the Brain"
Mr. Heenan is always impeccably dressed
With a style so distinctly urbane

And with every syllable out of his mouth
Comes a roar of sardonic approval
But in spite of his clever, quick-witted remarks
I'm impatient for his quick removal

KILLER KEN RESNICK

A couple words for "Killer Ken"
Whose hair is never out of place
And always wears a sunny smile
And tan upon his handsome face

He interviews the Wrestling Stars
Remaining dignified and cool
And those who try to match their wits
Could wind up looking like a fool

We watch Ken Resnick every week
But he is known as "Killer Ken"
'Cause he scores double figures
On our Killer scale from 1 to 10

HOWARD FINKEL AND MEL PHILLIPS

Here's to the Ring Announcers of the WWF
Howard Finkel and Mel Phillips are their names
Through every known distraction they have never
  missed a syllable
And every week they validate these claims

You know the wrestlers tend to be a bunch of
  rowdy characters
(They never give these men a moment's peace)
But the "Superstars of Wrestling" and the
  "Wrestling Challenge" programs
Have been graced with their announcing expertise

LORD ALFRED HAYES

From the British Aristocracy
Lord Alfred Hayes was born and bred
With scholastic honors from Oxford
And more distinctions left unsaid

It was his flair for unarmed combat
That led him to our Western shores
Where his sophisticated style
Would one day open other doors

The World Wrestling Federation
Assigned his Lordship to the mike
Where he could share with every fan
The witticisms that we like

The weekly feature called Update
And the magic of TNT
What this man has done for Wrestling
Is precisely our cup of tea!

CHAPTER 5

WRESTLING ARENAS

TORONTO MAPLE LEAF GARDENS

When I'm wrestling in Toronto
I remember all the greats
Frank Tunney and Lord Layton
Both have entered Heaven's gates

Then I think of Yukon Eric
Bunny Dunlap and the rest
Good just wasn't good enough
These fellows were the best

And Whipper Billy Watson?
He's still around today
When he was in his prime
He was the Hogan of his day

As we reap the fruits of their labors
Let no man ever forget
They bought our Canadian Whiskey
With their Canadian sweat

BOSTON GARDENS

The Boston Gardens is a place
   where history is made
The Glory of the Celtics
   and the Bruins shall not fade

I hear they're going to tear it down
   but that would be a crime
We'll take a cup of kindness yet
   for days of auld lang syne

You see the banners hanging
   from the rafters up above
Bostonians still look upon those
   artifacts with love

My name is Leaping Lanny
   and I'm very proud to say
I've been to Boston Gardens
   Massachusetts, USA

MADISON SQUARE GARDEN

I always hoped someday I'd get to wrestle at the
Garden
Well, in 1985 my dream came true
To all the Hulkamaniacs who made me feel so
welcome
I brought some extra frisbees just for you

PART TWO

OUT OF THE RING

CHAPTER 1

CHARITIES

George "The Animal" Steele

MUSCULAR DYSTROPHY

Hello wrestling fans, it's Leaping Lanny on the air
Full of World Wrestling Federation pride
We have formed a mighty tag-team with our friends
  at M.D.A.
And "ZETA 94.9" is on our side

Jerry Lewis has some kids who need your helping
  hand
And a miracle or two from up above
Every year his telethon reminds us we're a family
United by the healing bonds of love

Helping those less fortunate is never out of style
There's a human being in each wheelchair
Every dollar says "I love you" in a very special way
So dig down deep and show them that you care

It brings great satisfaction just to know you've done
  your best
For here on earth, God's work must be our own
When he sings his final song, let's all join in
  together
So one day, Jerry's kids can walk alone

SPECIAL OLYMPICS

It's called the Special Olympics
And there's something about that name
That's getting people off the bench
And putting them back in the game

No one should ever be denied
The chance to grab the center stage
Or share an honest open smile
With other boys and girls their age

For personal satisfaction
Or just having a little fun
The spirit of competition
Is the birthright of everyone

It's a very special moment
When they pass the torch and run
In the words of Charles Dickens
"God bless us everyone"

MULTIPLE SCLEROSIS

Cyndi Lauper's teaming up with Captain Lou Albano
The most unlikely pair you'll ever meet
They want to score a victory on multiple sclerosis
To get these people back up on their feet

Two million people suffer from this horrible disease
So don't just turn your head and walk away
We need your help to make this world a better
place to live
Please open up your heart and start today

DOMINICK DELLA ROCCA

This poem is dedicated to the Mayors of New York
Whose money, love, and time is their's to give
Inspired by the leadership of Mr. Della Rocca
They have made this world a better place to live

Imagine all the happiness they bring to boys and
girls
Who may not have had too much to smile about
But just knowing someone loves you in the spirit of
the Lord
Knocks the Devil out of sadness, fear, and doubt!

CHAPTER 2

CHILDREN'S HOSPITALS

BLYTHEDALE CHILDREN'S HOSPITAL

Blythedale Children's Hospital has everything they need
To help to heal the kids of every color, race, or creed

The Jewish philanthropic group of which they are a member
Brings Santa Claus eleven months a year besides December

JOHNS HOPKINS CHILDREN'S HOSPITAL

Johns Hopkins Children's Center is a family affair
You can feel the love on every single floor
The kids will leave, grow up, and come and visit
  every year
That's why it is the pride of Baltimore

From kidney transplantation to the simple common
  cold
They treat one hundred thousand kids a year
It's written on the faces of the boys and girls
  themselves
That God's alive and well and living here!

CHILDREN'S HOSPITAL OF BUFFALO

Children's Hospital of Buffalo
Is quite a special place
You'll find all that makes life beautiful
In each courageous face

There may be other hospitals
Of equal quality
But you must travel far to find
More hospitality!

ST. MARY'S

St. Mary's is a whole lot more
Than just a hospital for kids
It isn't big, but it's a cut above
There's only room for 95
But they serve more than medicine
Their menu has the precious gift of love

CHAPTER 3

SILLY STUFF

BREAKING THE ICE FOR BIG BROTHERS

Nobody said I *had* to skate at Rockefeller Plaza
Big Brothers only wanted me to come
But I weighed the thrill of doing things I'd never done before
Against the fear of really looking dumb

Jo Jo Starbuck and Ken Shelley gave me lots of fast advice
While my wife forcasted broken bones and stitches
When I fell down and broke my crown the audience went crazy

'Cause it *looked* like Leaping Lanny wet his britches!

FINANCIAL ADVICE

You want to double your investment
In the shortest possible time?
I'll give you some financial advice
Just fold your money neatly in half
And put it back in your pocket
And let the other suckers roll the dice.

SMOKING SUCKS

A cigarette smoker named "Clyde"
Thought all of those doctors had lied
He smoked one at a time
And he got along fine
Until quite prematurely he died

ODE TO LARRY "BUD" MELLMAN

If Larry "Bud" Mellman is the greatest of them all
He has only David Letterman to thank
It doesn't matter if we're laughing at the "Bud" or with him
Just as long as he is laughing to the bank

He has a little trouble with the cue cards now and then
His nails must be bitten to the quick
If I could put my finger on the key to his success
He personifies the "Stupid Human Trick"

THE GREASEMAN

When I'm in Baltimore or Washington I start the
day off right
With a little help from D.C. 101
If you're ever in that area, you must check out the
Greaseman
With his raunchy and irreverant brand of fun

I know some people want to take the Greaseman
off the air
But I return their good intentions with a scoff
Or to use a little esoteric Greaseman terminology
Perhaps you folks should all go "hobble off!"

BATH BEACH HEALTH SPA

I used to train at Bath Beach Health Spa
For a couple hundred reasons
But there's only room right now for just a few
It's Sue and Lou and Mary Ellen
John and Mike and Ralph and Brian
Frank and Donna, Dave and Tony, (Gina too)

INAPPROPRIATE BEHAVIOR

With subjects such as nudity
There is no "right" or "wrong"
Because taking off your clothes is not a sin
Right or wrong is not the issue
When you let it all hang out
It's deciding what's "appropriate" or "in"

WHO'S BEEN STEALING ALL THE CARDBOARD HULKSTERS?

One day, while at the airport, reading USA Today
I saw a picture of the Hulkster with his friends at "Circle K"
Throughout the country all his life-size posters disappeared
And considering their size, you must admit that's pretty weird

I know the Hulkster's fans would never shoplift, steal, or rob
So I speculate this crime would have to be an inside job
To all cashiers and employees: Come clean, or else resign
RETURN YOUR STOLEN HULK! (and I in turn will give back mine!)

HOW TO PRODUCE A RHYME ABUSE CABOOSE (OR HOW I ALMOST LOST MY POETIC LICENSE)

My favorite author, Dr. Seuss
Once taught a class in Rhyme Abuse
I'd like to try to put to use
The things I learned at Syracuse

I studied Hercules and Zeus
And articles by Claire Booth Luce
I learned an ace can beat a deuce
And twenty ways to cook a goose

I learned the way to tie a noose
To hang around, or just hang loose
The rope is brown like apple juice
But turns my face a bright chartreuce

Now Greta Garbo's in recluse
And so is Bullwinkle the Moose
I haven't used seduce or spruce
But I am bored, so I'll vamoose

CHAPTER 4

SERIOUS STUFF

POSSIBILITY THINKING

I met a girl, 10 years old
She looked at me and said,
"My father moved away last year,
I wish that I was dead!"

"My mother's working very hard
To keep this family fed,
I take care of my two sisters
And I wish that I was dead!"

I told her that I read a book
And every word is true
It said that tough times never last
Tough little girls do

It was only two years later
I saw that girl again
But she was not the tragic case
She was when she was 10

She has a brand new daddy
And a different point of view
And everyday she thanks the Lord
And Robert Schuller too!

MAY 12, 1987

I just met Robert Schuller
The handshake and the smile
The presence of sincerity
The absence of beguile

The silver hair and glasses
The sixty years of youth
The lifelong love of Jesus
His wisdom and His truth

I had to wait forever
But I didn't mind a bit
It was a day the Lord had made
And I was glad in it!

"B.T." MIKE MILLER
TEENAGE MR. KENTUCKY 1982

I was in the audience in 1982
My friend "B.T." was up there on the stage
Four trophies and a memory is all he still has left
For now his life has turned another page

A building he was working on collapsed and
  crushed his legs
He has to pick another wedding day
But Mike will never have to face the music all alone
He has his family, friends, and fiance

Geri is the girl he loves, and she won't leave his
  side
For loyalty, you couldn't ask for more
True love can overcome the greatest obstacles of
  life
Remember F.D.R. and Eleanor!

CHILD FIND

We are the "Friends of Child Find"
And everyone's responsible
We won't give up, no matter what the cost
If you spot a missing child
Help is just a call away
Remember: 1-800-I AM LOST

HONEST ABE

He failed at everything he tried
But always tried and tried again
And when he failed he tried and tried some more
His persistence saved our country
Through a time of desperation
Pitting brothers vs. brother in a war

But when he won his victory
He used the healing power of love
Not malice, but with charity for all
He brought the South up off her knees
And gave her back her dignity
We've never had a president so tall

He's a city in Nebraska
He's a tunnel in New York
A memorial in Washington D.C.
You can see him at Mt. Rushmore
And the penny and the five
And the pages from a time in history

Born in Hodenville, Kentucky
Made his name in Illinois
But an actor's bullet blew it all away
Mine eyes have seen the glory
Of the coming of the Lord
And the man who lived to save the U.S.A.

RICHARD NIXON

When Richard Nixon left the White House
In mass humiliation
He kept his head up high and shoulders broad
He had his family right beside him
Loyal in his rise and fall
And for that I'd like to stand up and applaud

Yes, there was Pat, and Trish, and Julie
They were there in '68
And they wouldn't leave his side when he was down
We sure do miss you Mr. Nixon
Because we are all so perfect
That we need someone like you to kick around

RONALD REAGAN

We voted twice for Ronald Reagan
And as history will tell
He was as tough as Harry Truman
When he had to give 'em hell

He faced cancer and a bullet wound
And beat them with a smile
And his toughest critics couldn't cramp
That Ronald Reagan style

He went from lifeguard to announcer
To the halls of Notre Dame
And when "The Gipper" leaves the White House
He will not go out in shame

He'll take his favorite leading lady
For a final curtain call
And the bells will ring for liberty
And justice for us all!

FREDDIE PRINZE

Freddie Prinze, the shooting star
Came too soon and went too far
All the world was at his door
Had it all, but needed more

All the snowblind actors know
Easy come and easy go
Living fast, but lost control
Gained the world, but lost his soul

Songs of love and joys of spring
Money buys you everything
Everything but peace of mind
That line should be underlined

Sell out crowds, but all alone
Lost his baby, wife and home
Visitation rights denied
Final chapter: suicide

The laughter died in sorrow
And so we face tomorrow
Success is one thing, brother
Happiness is quite another

ATTITUDE

Two prisoners, the story goes
Were looking out their window
But one of them could only see the bars
The other man with equal choice
And equal opportunity
Was raptured by the beauty of the stars

Circumstances notwithstanding
Do not make or break a man
But rather it's the other way around
A man can make his circumstance
Although he's trapped in bondage
Provided that his attitude is sound

DOGS

The death of a dog is the loss of a friend
You can never completely replace
Your memories linger of happier days
And the joy of that bright, fuzzy face

Though others forsake you, you're never alone
When the four-legged monster's in town
A Rover, a Fido, a Prince or a King
Sure can pick up a guy when he's down!

DADDY'S GIRL

Pretty little Lacy's in the springtime of her years
God's latest contribution to the dance
We are in the audience and she is on the stage
A relationship abundant with romance

But when she comes home to Florida she doesn't
have to dance
I've seen her daddy's heart swell up with pride
And for every single teardrop at the airport that may
fall
A couple hundred more are still inside

Time can be an enemy when she is not at home
He lives only for her visits and her calls
Even when she cannot hear through all of the
applause
He'll love her when the final curtain falls

THE POLICEMAN

He never gets the credit
He only takes the blame
Everywhere he goes
It's always more of the same
When layman meets policeman
You know that it's a fact
They smile at his face
And call him "pig" behind his back

He's the man who walks the beat
When you see him on the street
Tell him thanks because he has
A thankless job with little pay
You think that he's a big disgrace
With his nightstick and his mace
But he's a servant of the people
And he proves it everyday

While we sing for unsung heroes
Let us not forget his wife
Every waking hour she is
Fearing for his life
Through loneliness and worry
She does what she must do
A sacrifice she makes
While he's protecting me and you!

You talk of bribes, corruption
And police brutality
It paints an ugly picture
And reflects on you and me
You condemn the whole police force
For what one man does alone
If there's a perfect man among you
Let him cast a righteous stone

Remember this cause while you're
Putting down the man in blue
The next ungrateful life he saves
Might very well be you
Now my testimonial
Is coming to an end
I hope that it reminds you
The policeman is your friend

TO THE VIET NAM VETERAN

Theirs was not to reason why
Theirs was but to do or die
Their country needed them so off they went
They did not return in glory
For this was another story
"The Viet Nam American lament"

For all of those who gave their lives
Their parents, children, and their wives
They didn't get a thing that they deserved
These men were just as much and more
Than those from any other war
Don't let old soldiers pass by unobserved

ALICIA DAVIS

Alicia Davis left Kentucky many years ago
To sing in New York City was her dream
So many times they've told her "Don't call us, kid,
we'll call you . . ."
She has a fluctuating self-esteem

Alicia Davis types 140 words a minute
Fast enough to pay for groceries, gas, and rent
She supports a cat named Rudi, and a borderline
career
But it's not too long before her money's spent

I feel she has the talent and the guts to be a star
I know that she'll be fighting 'til the end
Someday this world is going to hear Alicia Davis
sing
But I'm already proud to be her friend

BOYD PIERCE: TEXAD SPECIALTY CO.

When Boyd Pierce gets down to business
He has so much ambition
He doesn't care what others do
He IS the competition

While others give us less for more
He gives us more for less
That's why I'm a happy client
And he's such a big success!

TONY

I have a friend from Downers Grove
Who had a younger brother
(He passed away when he was only ten)
Everybody's faith was tested
Not the least of which was mine
Our lives would never be the same again

If God was so all powerful
Like everybody told me
Then tell me why he took that little guy
The years can't heal the broken hearts
His family copes with every day
For they'll remember Tony 'til they die

That is when they'll be together
With an everlasting joy
That will far surpass their sorrow here on earth
I cannot prove a word I say
But I believe with all my heart
That death is just God's way of giving birth

THAT SPECIAL LIST

They laughed at Thomas Edison
And Christopher Columbus
They laughed at Alexander Graham Bell
When Galileo's telescope
Put old beliefs in orbit
They made his family's life a living hell

They had their laugh at Kitty Hawk
'til things got off the ground
They used to say that both the Wrights were wrong
Clark Gable's ears were much to big to ever be a
star
And Jackie Robinson did not belong

If anybody laughs at you
You really should be flattered
Your name is on a very special list
If things don't look so good right now
Hang on a little longer
Some frogs don't look so good until they're kissed

OPRAH WINFREY

From child abuse, to broken home, to battle of the bulge
Self-pity is one sport that Oprah Winfrey won't indulge

She took the pieces of her life and put them back together
She'd rather dam the flood than bitch and moan about the weather

If pretty is as pretty does, Oh mirror on the wall
Then "Chocolate Cream" (and not "Snow White") is fairest of them all

JUST SAY NO

When I was fourteen years of age
A "party" invitation
Made me shave three tiny whiskers from my face
When I arrived a little late
The smell of marijuana
Made me look and feel completely out of place

But then I saw that pretty girl
From Mrs. Fisher's Spanish class
She smiled at me and offered me some smoke
When I refused I heard a voice
Which triggered off some laughter
So guess who was the victim of the joke

I don't recall who wrote the line
"Faint heart ne'er won fair lady"
But this "lady" kept on offering her weed
But I just kept on saying no
And much to my amazement
Some other kids were following my lead

So even though I'm older now
The story's not much different
Than the way things were so many years ago
The key to popularity
Is how much you love others
But never be afraid to tell them NO

CHAPTER 5

MY PRIVATE COLLECTION

"JYD" (Junkyard Dog)

GUSTO GIRL

You turn my early Monday mornings
into Saturday night
You pour gusto on an ordinary day
The colors that you've shown me
are as hard to live without
As it is for me to tear myself away

Now I haven't shown you anything
you haven't seen before
The more you look, the less there is to see
The only time I'm anything is when
I am with you
I hope you feel the same when you're with me

But when I'm caught in the danger zone
of your contagious smile
I feel like Mickey Mantle in his prime
I'm the Spirit of St. Louis,
I'm the great Chicago Fire
I'm the New York Mets of 1969

It wasn't very long ago
I didn't know your name
Unenchanted by the magic of your eyes
It's too soon to say "I love you"
even though I know for sure
Here's to hoping that the feeling never dies

LOVE ME DUST

If they invented "love me" dust
I'd buy myself a ton
I'd dump the whole supply on you
And then we'd have some fun

You'd look at me through different eyes
And I'd enjoy the view
But I don't need a speck of dust
To tell me I love you

DELIVERANCE

It was in my darkest hour with the devil at my door
And an emptiness within that cried out low
I felt the presence of my Lord deliver me from evil
When I thought I had no other place to go

He said "I've let you have your fun, but now the party's over
You found pleasure wasn't pleasing after all
If you would trust me and obey you'll go from rags to riches
If you bear my cross I'll have you walking tall"

The Holy Spirit came to me and filled me with such power
That I knew what Jesus wanted with my life
So I picked up the telephone and followed HIS instructions
And I asked the girl I loved to be my wife!

MAGEN

The nurse tells me to leave the room
So they can put Sally under
The doctor spares my lonesome gloom
And shows me God's little wonder

I see my daughter through the glass
But now I have some calls to make
"Good news, we have a little lass"
(A miracle, for goodness sake)

Now Sally's mom and I go home
But who can sleep on such a night
With wife and baby all alone
Anxiety is only right

I wrestle with the words and rhyme
As Magen feeds at Sally's breast
I must be quick, it's almost time
To meet with "Grizzly" and the rest

When I return two days from now
I hope my little family's fine
My little Magen, I thee endow
With love, declare that you are mine!

OUR BABY GIRL

Our baby girl has just been born
We counted all her toes
She's a bundle of perfection
Like an early springtime rose

We hold our little miracle
And make this solemn vow
If we haven't praised the Lord before
We sure do praise him now

WEE CARE

Wee care for every Sam and Sue
And every Mark and Magen too
'Cause even though it's just a loan
We love them as our very own
And even when they scream and shout
They are what love is all about
And we have extra love to spare
We're in this business 'cause Wee Care

This poem was written for a day care center in Lexington, Kentucky called Wee Care

MAGEN'S CHOICE

Mr. Snuffle-upagus
Ernie, Bert, and Grover
And all the ones my daughter wants to meet
Now she knows her ABC's
And all her 1,2,3's
'Cause she knows how to get to Sesame Street

HIS BROTHER'S KEEPER

His teeth may be false, but his smile is for real
He is gray, but grown gracefully old
But Grizzly Smith means a lot more to me
Than a trunk full of silver and gold

For the endless miles I have spent in his car
In the time before Magen was born
He would laugh as I talked myself blue in the face
With his eyes weatherbeaten and worn

Then he gave me his classic Will Rogers approach
As he gently invaded my mind
I learned more from that big hulking giant of a man
Than from all of my teachers combined

The high price of wisdom is costly indeed
While foolishness buys and sells cheaper
What words best describe Mr. Grizzly Smith?
Let's just say he is HIS brother's keeper

GOOD NEIGHBORS

When I came back to Downers Grove
I looked at all the photographs of Kelly in the stages of her life
With Tom and Sandy older now and Kelly almost fully grown
I'm glad I have a daughter and a wife

'Cause life is full of emptiness with no one home to share your love
And freedom isn't really free at all
Everything we do is costly from the cradle to the grave
And every Spring and Summer has a Fall

What your mom and daddy gave to you was everything they had to give
But you have paid them back time after time
When you count your many blessings you should start with Tom and Sandy
And I'll begin with you when I count mine

MORE GOOD NEIGHBORS

Steve and Andi Giordano used to be our next door neighbors
When we lived on Staten Island, U.S.A.
Although we didn't stay too long, we still have happy memories
And I would like to think of them this way

Forever, Andi's in the bathroom always messing with her hair
While Steve is on the phone with business calls
Raven is their hyper-active dog who'll be remembered
For leaving all four footprints on the walls

Josie, Dottie, Nikki, Donna, Jane and Billy, Scott and Glory
Jerry, Stephanie and Justin and the rest
I was surprised to find the Eastern people every bit as friendly
As the people from the North and South and West!

MY FATHER BELIEVE IT OR NOT!

Three mats, all red from friction burn
Four hours of bloody tortured hell
But World's records aren't a piece of cake
6,000 situps won the crown
So why the extra 33
The media asked why for goodness sake

Yes, why indeed the 33
And what was the significance
And why did he go through that needless strife
That was my father on the mat
He did it all for Jesus Christ
Just one situp for each year of His life

TO MOM

I have a Jewish mother
Who made me go to school
In spite of my resistance
And I could be a mule

Through years of aggravation
(And she was stubborn too)
Although not always popular
That's what she had to do

The clock would tick by slowly
Oh, what a price to pay
I finally earned my freedom
On graduation day

Now that my book is finished
There's nothing left to do
But thank my Jewish mother
And tell her "I love you"